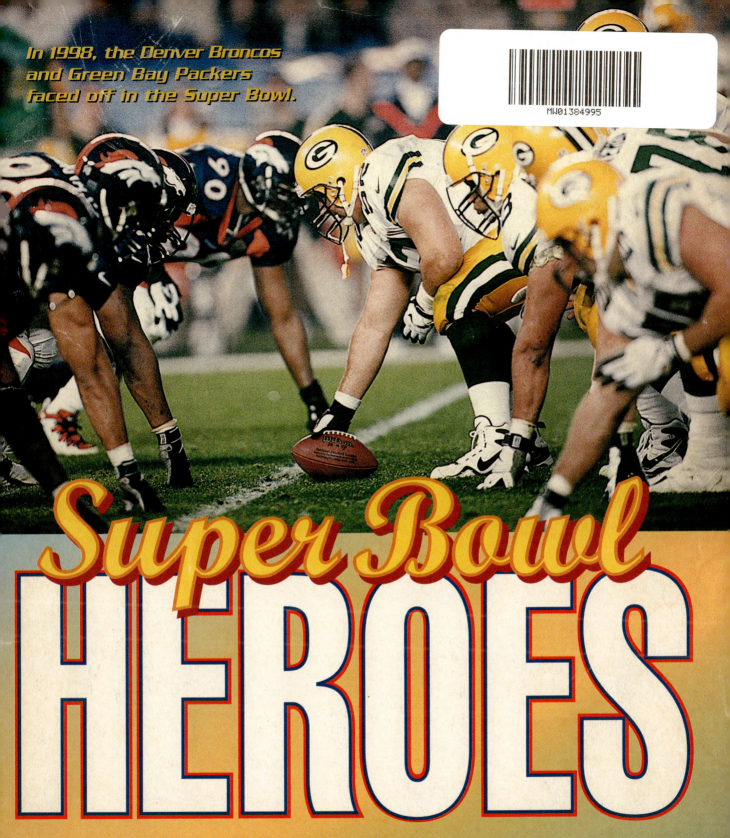

In 1998, the Denver Broncos and Green Bay Packers faced off in the Super Bowl.

Super Bowl HEROES

By Richard Deitsch

A SPORTS ILLUSTRATED For Kids Book

Terrell Davis ran away with the 1998 Super Bowl.

The winner gets the Vince Lombardi trophy.

CONTENTS

Super PLAYERS 4

Super TEAMS 22

Super MOMENTS 28

RODUCTION

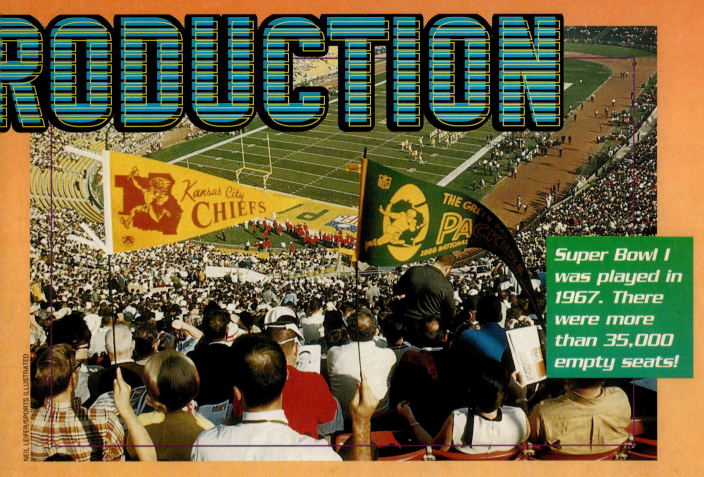

Super Bowl I was played in 1967. There were more than 35,000 empty seats!

Where were you on Super Bowl Sunday last January? If you are like millions of

other Americans, you were probably glued to your TV set. You were watching the American Football Conference champion battle the National Football Conference champion in the biggest game of all.

In 1998, you would have seen the terrific moves of Terrell Davis. The powerful running back helped the Denver Broncos defeat the Green Bay Packers, 31–24, in Super Bowl XXXII.

Yes, that's Super Bowl *32* (the NFL likes Roman numerals!). The very first Super Bowl was played on January 15, 1967. The Green Bay Packers beat the Kansas City Chiefs, 35–10. But that game wasn't called the Super Bowl. It was the AFL-NFL World Championship Game. The game was renamed the Super Bowl in 1969.

Over the years, there have been plenty of awesome stars and amazing moments in the Super Bowl. *Super Bowl Heroes* features super-passers such as Bart Starr and Brett Favre, and speedy runners such as Franco Harris and Marcus Allen. It replays Jerry Rice's spectacular catches and one of Joe Montana's sensational comebacks.

Super Bowl Heroes has all the plays covered. So sit back, relax, and get ready for some super football moments!

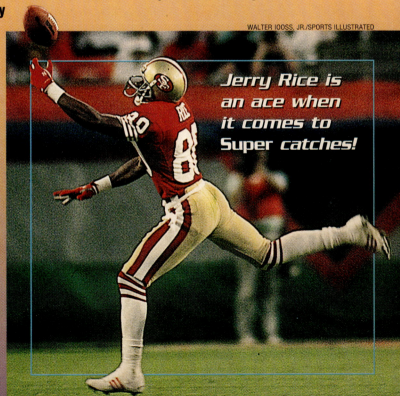

Jerry Rice is an ace when it comes to Super catches!

SUPER PLAYERS

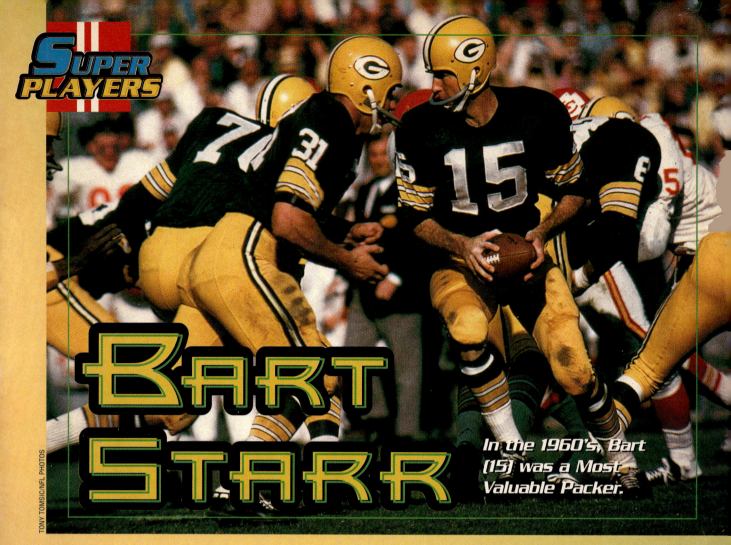

Bart Starr

In the 1960's, Bart (15) was a Most Valuable Packer.

Who could have predicted that Bart Starr would

become the leader of football's greatest dynasty? No one. Bart had been selected by the team in the 17th round of the 1956 NFL draft. When he arrived in training camp, he was given the number 42. (Quarterbacks usually get low numbers, like 8 or 12.) "It was obvious they thought I wasn't going to stay," says Bart.

As it turned out, Bart stayed for 16 years. His strong, steady play at quarterback helped the Packers win five titles in seven years during the 1960's.

But Bart really made his splash in the Super Bowl. On January 15, 1967, in the first Super Bowl game ever played, Bart was, well, super. He completed 16 of 23 passes for 250 yards and passed for two touchdowns in the Packers' 35–10 win over the Kansas City Chiefs. On third-down plays in the game, Bart completed a sparkling 10 of 13 passes. He was named the game's MVP.

"Bart called a perfect game," said wide receiver Max McGee.

The next year, Bart led the team back to the Super Bowl. Once again, he made all the right moves. In the second quarter, the Packers were leading the Oakland Raiders, 6–0. With 11:01 left in the quarter, Bart threw a pass to wide receiver Boyd Dowler for a 62-yard touchdown. The Packers went on to win the game, 33–14. Bart was named the game's MVP once again.

So whatever happened to the number 42 jersey? Shortly after Bart made the team, he was assigned the number 15. *That* number was retired by Green Bay in 1973.

SCOUTING REPORT

Born: January 9, 1934, in Montgomery, Alabama
Career Stats: Completed 57.4 percent of his passes for 152 TDs in 16 seasons (1956-71). Led Packers to five NFL titles.
Super Bowl Stats: Completed 29 of 47 passes for 452 yards and three TDs.
Fast Fact: Bart and Pittsburgh Steeler quarterback Terry Bradshaw are the only players to be named MVP in back-to-back Super Bowls.

Joe Namath

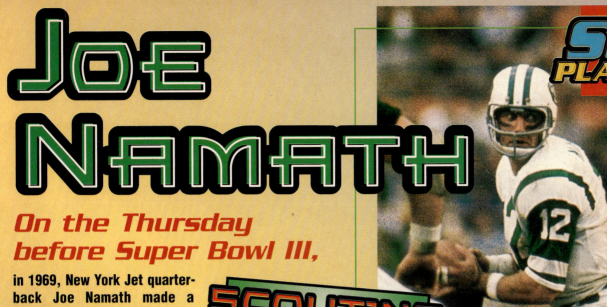

"Broadway Joe" put on quite a passing show in Super Bowl III.

On the Thursday before Super Bowl III, in 1969, New York Jet quarterback Joe Namath made a shocking boast: "The Jets will win on Sunday," said Joe. "I guarantee it."

Was Joe crazy? Many fans believed the Baltimore Colts could not be beaten. The Colts had finished the regular season with a 13–1 record. Also, the Colts were a part of the powerful National Football League while the Jets were part of the newer American Football League. In 1970, the two leagues would merge to form one giant league, but at the time, the two leagues were rivals. The NFL thought it was superior to the AFL. And the NFL's teams had beaten the AFL teams in the two previous Super Bowls by a combined score of 68–24!

Those who knew Joe weren't surprised by his boast. He was a bold young guy who liked to say what was on his mind. "I assure you that the Colts have never had to play against the quarterbacks like we have in the AFL," Joe said.

When the game began, the Jets shocked the Colts by scoring first. They ran the ball right into the Colts defense. When they weren't running the ball, Joe was throwing short passes. The Jets led 7–0 at halftime and 16–0 by the fourth quarter. The Colts scored a late touchdown, but it was hardly enough. The Jets would go on to a 16–7 upset.

Joe completed 17 of 28 passes for 206 yards in the game. But it was his boast, and the fact that he made good on it, that made him famous.

Scouting Report

Born: May 31, 1943, in Beaver Falls, Pennsylvania

Career Stats: Completed 50 percent of passes for 173 TDs in 13 seasons (1965-77) with the Jets and Rams. Led the NFL in TD passes in 1972 with 19.

Super Bowl Stats: Completed 17 of 28 passes for 206 yards and no interceptions.

Fast Fact: Joe was the first quarterback in history to pass for 4,000 or more yards in a season. He threw for 4,007 yards in 1967.

Quick Kicks

Neon Namath Joe was nicknamed "Broadway Joe," after the famous street, because he enjoyed the nightlife in New York.

What A Month On October 15, 1967, Joe tied an AFL record by being intercepted six times in one game. Over the next two weeks, he tied an AFL record with 15 straight completions.

TV Star After his career was over, Joe acted in TV shows, movies, and the theater.

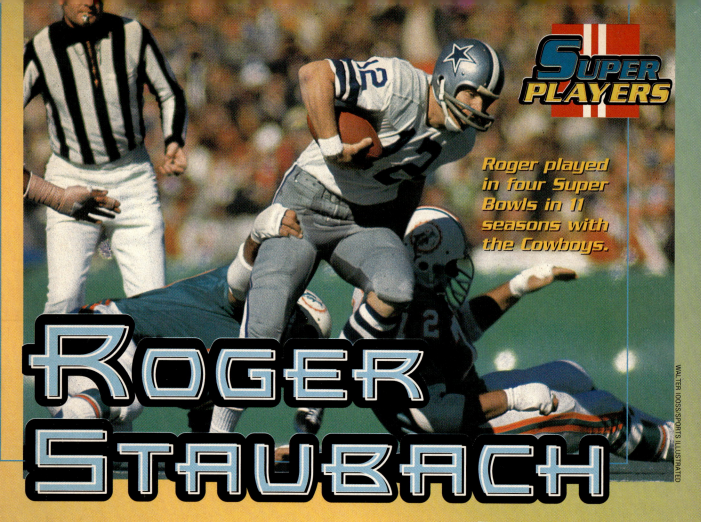

SUPER PLAYERS

Roger played in four Super Bowls in 11 seasons with the Cowboys.

WALTER IOOSS/SPORTS ILLUSTRATED

ROGER STAUBACH

The Dallas Cowboys had to

wait for Roger Staubach. They drafted him in the 10th round of the 1964 NFL draft. But they didn't get him until 1969. Roger had one more year to go at the United States Naval Academy. Then he had to serve in the Navy for four years before he could play pro football.

So the Cowboys waited.

Even after he had joined the team, the Cowboys waited. Roger didn't play much until 1971, but then, *did he play!* That season, at the ripe old age of 29, Roger threw 15 touchdowns and only four interceptions. He was named the NFL's Player of the Year.

Roger also led the Cowboys to a 24–3 victory over the Miami Dolphins in Super Bowl VI (1972). Despite bruising his ribs, Roger completed 12 of 19 passes for 119 yards and three touchdowns! He didn't throw a single interception and was named the game's Most Valuable Player.

Roger led the Cowboys to three more Super Bowls. In 1978, Dallas met the Denver Broncos in Super Bowl XII. Roger completed 17 of 25 passes for 183 yards and one touchdown. The Cowboys cruised to a 27–10 win.

In 1979, Roger played in his last Super Bowl. He was matched against terrific quarterback Terry Bradshaw *(see page 8)* of the Pittsburgh Steelers. Roger threw three touchdowns passes in that game, but Terry threw four. The Steelers won, 35–31

Even though the Cowboys had to wait for Roger to join them at first, they were glad to have this Navy man at the helm!

SCOUTING REPORT

Born: February 5, 1942, in Cincinnati, Ohio

Career Stats: Completed 57 percent of his passes for 153 TDs in 11 seasons (1969-79) with the Dallas Cowboys. Named to six Pro Bowls. Inducted into the Hall of Fame in 1985.

Super Bowl Stats: Completed 61 of 98 passes for 734 yards and eight TDs in four games (1972, '76, '78, and '79). Named MVP of Super Bowl VI (1972).

Cool Fact: Roger was nicknamed Captain Comeback. During his career, the Cowboys rallied to win 23 games that they had been losing in the fourth quarter!

SUPER PLAYERS

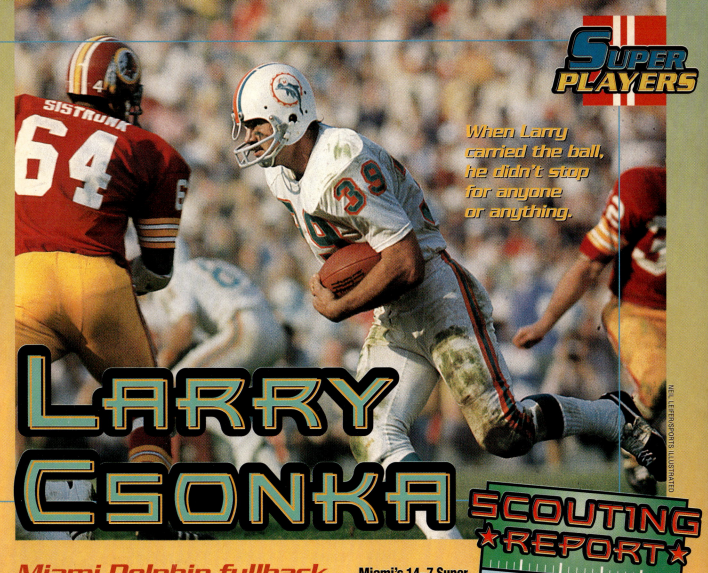

When Larry carried the ball, he didn't stop for anyone or anything.

LARRY CSONKA

SCOUTING REPORT

Born: December 25, 1946, in Stow, Ohio

Career Stats: Rushed for 8,081 yards and scored 68 TDs with the Miami Dolphins and New York Giants (1968-79). Inducted into the Hall of Fame in 1987.

Super Bowl Stats: Rushed 57 times for 297 yards and two TDs in three games (1972, '73, '74). Named MVP of '74 game.

Cool Fact: With 1,891 carries and 106 receptions in his career, Larry fumbled only 21 times.

Miami Dolphin fullback Larry Csonka wasn't a pretty runner. He was more like a human wrecking ball. He simply ran *through* people in his way.

Zonk (Larry's last name was pronounced *ZONK-ah*) helped the Dolphins make history. Miami went 17–0 in the 1972 season and won Super Bowl VII to become the only undefeated team in NFL history. Zonk rushed for 112 yards on 15 carries in Miami's 14–7 Super Bowl victory over Washington.

The next year, against the Minnesota Vikings in Super Bowl VIII, Zonk played even better. On the first drive, he carried the ball five times for 36 yards, including a five-yard TD run. He finished with 33 carries for two touchdowns and 145 yards. His 145 yards were twice as much as the entire Viking team had and set a Super Bowl record.

After the game, Minnesota quarterback Fran Tarkenton put it well. "Larry Csonka's the strongest fullback I've ever seen," he said.

QUICK KICKS

Double Trouble
Only two running backs have run for more than 100 yards in back-to-back Super Bowl games: Larry and Emmitt Smith *(page 15)* of the Dallas Cowboys.

Number Two
Franco Harris *(page 9)* is the only player to rush for more yards than Larry in Super Bowl play. Franco gained 354 yards in four Super Bowls. Larry had 297 yards in three games.

TERRY BRADSHAW

SUPER PLAYERS

Quarterback Terry Bradshaw led the Pittsburgh Steelers to the Super Bowl four times between 1975 and 1980. They won every time! Only one other quarterback *(see "Joe Montana," page 10)* led his team to four Super Bowl victories. But Terry was the one who did it first!

Terry had a great arm. He averaged 11.1 yards per pass in Super Bowl play. That's the highest yards-per-pass of any Super Bowl quarterback.

"Terry throws a football twenty yards like I throw a dart fifteen feet," said Dallas Cowboy safety Charlie Waters.

The Steelers won back-to-back Super Bowls in 1975 and 1976. Terry threw the winning TD pass to wide receiver Lynn Swann *(page 29)* in 1976. But in Pittsburgh's second pair of titles, Terry really shone. He was MVP of both games!

In Super Bowl XIII (1979), Terry completed 17 of 30 passes for 318 yards and four TDs. He threw three TDs in the first half alone! The Steelers beat the Cowboys, 35–31.

The next year, Terry passed for 309 yards. Pittsburgh beat the Los Angeles Rams, 31–19, in Super Bowl XIV.

At his 1989 induction to Pro Football's Hall of Fame, Terry said, "I want to be remembered as a winner." Don't worry!

SCOUTING REPORT

Born: September 2, 1948, in Shreveport, Louisiana

Career Stats: Completed 51.9 percent of his passes for 212 TDs in 14 seasons (1970-83) with the Pittsburgh Steelers. Inducted into the Hall of Fame in 1989.

Super Bowl Stats: Completed 49 of 84 passes for 932 yards and nine TDs in four games (1975, '76, '79, and '80). Named MVP of 1979 and '80 games.

Cool Fact: Terry co-hosts the *Fox NFL Sunday* show on TV.

Terry handed the Steelers four Super Bowl titles!

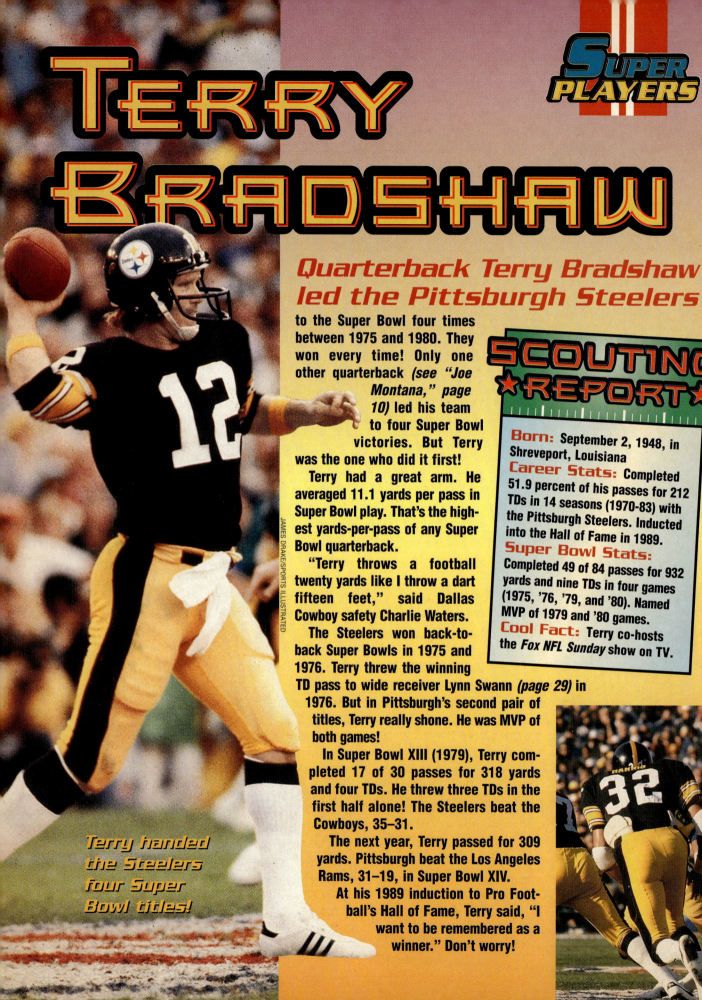

FRANCO HARRIS

SUPER PLAYERS

In the days just before Super Bowl IX (1975), Pittsburgh Steeler running back Franco Harris had a bad head cold. But that didn't prevent him from rushing 34 times for 158 yards — and setting two Super Bowl records — to lead the Steelers to a 16–6 victory over the Minnesota Vikings.

Franco's performance broke the record for most rushing yards in one Super Bowl that Larry Csonka *(see page 7)* had set in Super Bowl VIII. Franco's 34 carries set the Super Bowl record for most carries in a game. (Both records have since been broken.)

Franco's running was the key to the Steeler victory. Early in the third quarter, Franco scored on a nine-yard TD run to give Pittsburgh a 9–0 lead. In the fourth quarter, he carried the ball 12 times for 40 yards. That helped keep the ball away from the Viking offense. Franco carried the ball six times on Pittsburgh's next-to-last drive, which led to a TD.

Franco was always ready when the Steelers needed a big play. In Super Bowl XIII (1979), he put the game away with a 22-yard fourth-quarter touchdown run against the Dallas Cowboys. In Super Bowl XIV (1980), he scored two TDs against the Los Angeles Rams. Franco helped Pittsburgh win the Super Bowl four times in six years! Through the 1998 game, Franco has more carries and yards in the Super Bowl than any other running back.

Hall of Fame running back Jim Brown once said, "If I were starting a team and could choose any running back to build my backfield around, I'd pick Franco." Pittsburgh did!

SCOUTING REPORT

Born: March 7, 1950, in Fort Dix, New Jersey

Career Stats: Rushed for 12,120 yards and 91 TDs in 13 seasons (1972-84) with the Pittsburgh Steelers and Seattle Seahawks. Inducted into the Hall of Fame (1990).

Super Bowl Stats: Rushed 101 times for 354 yards and four TDs in four games (1975, '76, '79, '80). Named '75 MVP.

Cool Fact: Franco was also a great receiver! He caught 307 passes for 2,287 yds. and nine TDs!

Franco, known for rushing, was also a good receiver.

JOHN IACONO/SPORTS ILLUSTRATED

QUICK KICKS

Yard Man Franco rushed for 1,000 or more yards in a season eight times in his career.

Mr. TD Only Emmitt Smith has rushed for more TDs (five) in Super Bowl play than Franco.

Good Start Franco was the Steelers' first-round draft pick. In his rookie season, he gained 1,055 yards on 188 carries. He scored 11 touchdowns. Ten of them were rushing TDs.

JOHN IACONO/SPORTS ILLUSTRATED

SUPER PLAYERS

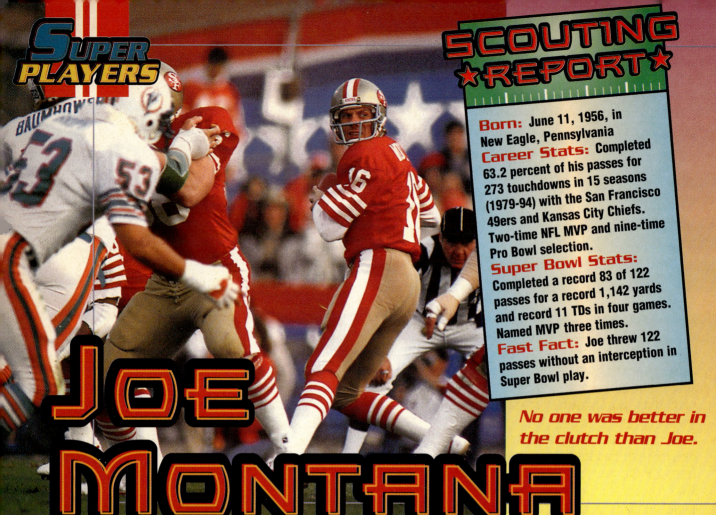

RONALD C. MODRA/SPORTS ILLUSTRATED

JOE MONTANA

SCOUTING REPORT

Born: June 11, 1956, in New Eagle, Pennsylvania

Career Stats: Completed 63.2 percent of his passes for 273 touchdowns in 15 seasons (1979-94) with the San Francisco 49ers and Kansas City Chiefs. Two-time NFL MVP and nine-time Pro Bowl selection.

Super Bowl Stats: Completed a record 83 of 122 passes for a record 1,142 yards and record 11 TDs in four games. Named MVP three times.

Fast Fact: Joe threw 122 passes without an interception in Super Bowl play.

No one was better in the clutch than Joe.

QUICK

Joe Montana earned the nickname Joe Cool because he stayed calm under pressure. The bigger the game, the better he played. And nowhere was he cooler than in the biggest game of all: The Super Bowl!

Joe led the San Francisco 49ers to four Super Bowl victories between 1982 and 1990. But his greatest display of cool and talent came in Super Bowl XXIII, when he directed an amazing fourth-quarter drive.

The 49ers were trailing the Cincinnati Bengals, 16–13, with just over three minutes left to play. The 49ers got the ball on their own eight-yard line. To win the game, they would have to move the ball 92 yards. That seemed impossible. But Joe, as always, was ready for the challenge. "Let's go, be tough," he told his teammates.

Joe completed three straight passes for 22 yards. Seven plays later, there was 1:17 left in the game. Joe threw a 27-yard pass to wide receiver Jerry Rice, who was stopped on the Bengals' 18-yard line.

Two plays later, Joe threw the game-winning pass to wide receiver John Taylor in the back of the Bengal end zone. *Score!* And there were only 34 seconds left on the clock. Joe and the 49ers had come back to win, 20–16. It was the first time a Super Bowl had been won with a touchdown so late in the game.

Joe won his fourth and final Super Bowl championship the next year. It was a 55–10 blowout over the Denver Broncos in Super Bowl XXIV. Joe completed 22 of 29 passes for 297 yards and five touchdowns. He was named the Super Bowl MVP — for the third time! Joe is the only three-time Super Bowl MVP in NFL history.

Perfect Over the course of two games in 1987, Joe completed an NFL-record 22 passes in a row.

The 400 Club Joe passed for 400 yards in a game seven times during his career. Only Dan Marino has had more 400-yard passing games (13).

Super Stuff Joe holds the record for most yards gained in a Super Bowl. He threw for 357 yards against the Bengals in Super Bowl XXIII. He also holds the record for most Super Bowl touchdown passes (11).

JERRY RICE

Who is the best wide receiver in

Super Bowl history? You better believe it's Jerry Rice of the San Francisco 49ers. Jerry holds or shares 10 Super Bowl records. No one has scored more touchdowns (he has seven) or more receptions (28) in Super Bowl play than the fleet-footed receiver with great hands.

Jerry's performance against the Cincinnati Bengals in 1989's Super Bowl XXIII was probably the greatest by a wide receiver in Super Bowl history. It was also the most unlikely. Jerry had sprained his ankle a week before the game and wasn't sure if he would be able to play at full strength. He shouldn't have worried. Jerry caught 11 passes for 215 yards and scored one touchdown. Nine catches gave the 49ers first downs. Five catches came in the fourth quarter when the 49ers came from behind, 16–13, to beat the Bengals, 20–16.

Jerry was nearly as good the next year, against the Denver Broncos in Super Bowl XXIV. He caught seven passes for 148 yards and three touchdowns in the 49ers' 55–10 win.

Quarterback Joe Montana threw all those passes to Jerry. But Joe left the team and went to the Kansas City Chiefs after the 1992 season. How would Jerry do with Steve Young, the quarterback who took over the team? Just great!

Three years later, in Super Bowl XXIX, Jerry caught 10 passes for 149 yards and three more touchdowns! The 49ers beat the San Diego Chargers, 49–26.

"Jerry Rice with one arm [would be] better than everyone in the league with two arms," Steve said after the game.

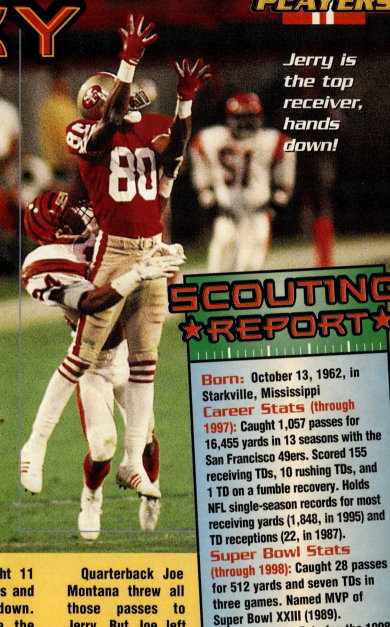

Jerry is the top receiver, hands down!

RONALD C. MODRA/SPORTS ILLUSTRATED

SUPER PLAYERS

SCOUTING REPORT

Born: October 13, 1962, in Starkville, Mississippi

Career Stats (through 1997): Caught 1,057 passes for 16,455 yards in 13 seasons with the San Francisco 49ers. Scored 155 receiving TDs, 10 rushing TDs, and 1 TD on a fumble recovery. Holds NFL single-season records for most receiving yards (1,848, in 1995) and TD receptions (22, in 1987).

Super Bowl Stats (through 1998): Caught 28 passes for 512 yards and seven TDs in three games. Named MVP of Super Bowl XXIII (1989).

Fast Fact: Entering the 1998 season, Jerry was the NFL's all-time leader in TDs, pass receptions, and receiving yards.

One Man Show Jerry has had 1,000 or more receiving yards in a season 11 times.

TD After TD From December 19, 1986, to December 27, 1987, Jerry caught one or more touchdown passes in 13 straight games. That's the NFL record for consecutive games with a TD reception!

Mr. 100 Jerry has had 100 or more receiving yards in a game 61 times.

Pro of Pros Jerry has been selected to the Pro Bowl 11 times in his 13-season career.

SUPER PLAYERS

Phil Simms

Just how good was starting

New York Giant quarterback Phil Simms against the Denver Broncos in Super Bowl XXI in 1987? He was nearly perfect. In fact, his performance may have been the greatest by a quarterback in Super Bowl history.

Phil completed 22 of 25 passes. His pinpoint passing led the Giants to a 39–20 victory and their first championship since 1956.

With his team leading 19–10 in the third quarter, Phil used a trick play called "the fleaflicker" to put the game away. It was second down, with six yards to go from the Denver 45. Phil handed off to running back Joe Morris. But Joe then pitched the ball right *back* to Phil! So Phil threw a 44-yard pass to wide receiver Phil McConkey. A play later, the Giants led, 26–10.

Phil completed eight passes for 123 yards and threw for a touchdown in that amazing quarter. "I was like a fastball pitcher," said Phil. "Almost every pass landed exactly where I wanted it to."

Giant coach Bill Parcells said, "Phil quarterbacked as good a game as ever has been played."

Phil led the Giants to victory in their very first Super Bowl!

JOHN IACONO/SPORTS ILLUSTRATED

SCOUTING REPORT

Born: November 3, 1955, in Lebanon, Kentucky

Career Stats: Completed 55.4 percent of passes for 157 touchdowns in 14 seasons (1979-93) with the New York Giants. Named to the Pro Bowl twice.

Super Bowl Stats: Completed 22 of 25 passes for 268 yards and three touchdowns in one game. Named MVP of Super Bowl XXI (1987).

Cool Fact: Phil holds 15 New York Giant passing records.

QUICK

Mr. Perfect Phil holds the Super Bowl record for highest completion percentage in one game (88 percent).

In a Row Against the Broncos, Phil completed 10 passes in a row. Only Joe Montana has completed more passes in a row in a Super Bowl game (13).

Hurray! In 1981, Phil led the Giants to the playoffs for the first time in 18 seasons. He led them back to the playoffs in three of the next five seasons. In 1987, he guided them to their first Super Bowl.

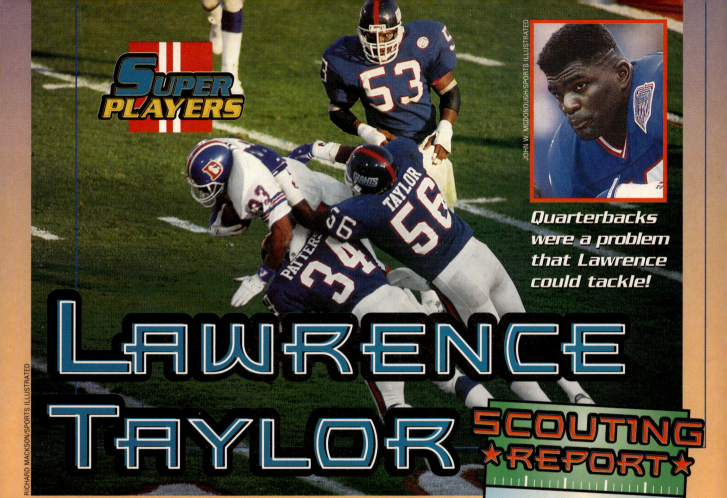

SUPER PLAYERS

Quarterbacks were a problem that Lawrence could tackle!

LAWRENCE TAYLOR

SCOUTING REPORT

Born: February 4, 1959, in Williamsburg, Virginia

Career Stats: Had 132.5 quarterback sacks and nine interceptions in 13 seasons (1981-93) with the New York Giants. Named to 10 Pro Bowls.

Super Bowl Stats: Led Giant defense to wins in Super Bowl XXI (1987) and XXV (1991). Had five tackles in the two games.

Cool Fact: Lawrence's jersey, number 56, was retired at Giants Stadium in 1994.

KICKS

Sack-Man I
Lawrence set a team record in the 1986 season with 20.5 sacks, the third-highest single-season sack total in NFL history.

Sack-Man II
Lawrence had more than 10 sacks in seven of his 13 NFL seasons. And it was seven seasons in a row!

New Slot Lawrence played tight end during a 1987 game.

Prince of Sacks
Lawrence retired in 1993, second in sacks on the NFL's all-time list (132.5).

New York Giant

Linebacker Lawrence Taylor terrorized NFL quarterbacks, running backs, and receivers for 13 seasons. LT, as he was known, was fast enough to run down the speediest receivers. He was strong enough to push aside 300-pound linemen. Trying to block him gave opposing coaches a major headache.

In Super Bowl XXI, the Denver Broncos got an LT headache! LT had four tackles in that game, including a *huge* sack of Bronco quarterback John Elway. The Broncos were leading, 10–7, in the second quarter. They had moved the ball to the Giants' one-yard line, thanks to John's accurate passing. They were set to score!

The Broncos brought in their goal-line offense. They planned to run the ball in for a touchdown — and a 10-point lead. On first down, John ran a sweep to the right side (he ran to the right with blockers "sweeping" the way for him). But LT stopped John cold. Instead of moving one yard forward for a TD, John was pushed one yard back!

The Broncos tried to run again on the next two plays, but LT and his defensive teammates held tight. On fourth down, Denver kicker Rich Karlis missed the field goal.

The Giants took over the game. They scored 30 second-half points, a Super Bowl record, and won, 39–20. Afterward, LT appeared at a press conference wearing a Superman T-shirt. "The problem is," said LT, "sometimes it's hard to find a phone booth."

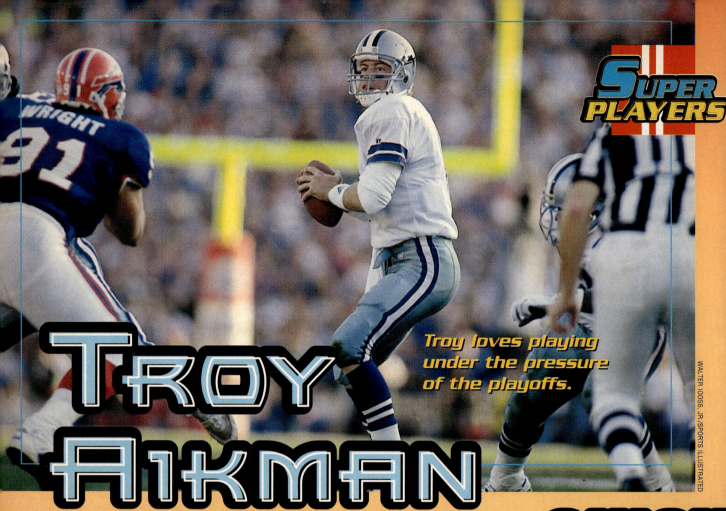

Troy loves playing under the pressure of the playoffs.

WALTER IOOSS, JR./SPORTS ILLUSTRATED

SUPER PLAYERS

TROY AIKMAN

Most quarterbacks would be happy

to lead their team to even one Super Bowl victory. But Troy Aikman helped the Dallas Cowboys win three! Only two other quarterbacks in NFL history have won more than three Super Bowl championships: Joe Montana *(see page 10)* and Terry Bradshaw *(page 8)* each have four. That's very good company!

Troy led the Cowboys to Super Bowl wins in 1993, 1994, and 1996. If he had to pick his favorite, it would probably be the first. Troy was terrific as Dallas beat the Buffalo Bills in Super Bowl XXVII, in Pasadena, California. He completed 22 of 30 passes for 273 yards. He threw four touchdown passes — and no interceptions. The Cowboys went on to a 52–17 win. Troy was just 26 years old. He was one of the youngest quarterbacks to win the Super Bowl *and* the MVP award!

In 1994, the Cowboys again defeated the Bills in the Super Bowl. Troy finished with 19 of 27 passes for 207 yards. In 1996, Dallas beat the Pittsburgh Steelers, 27–17. All told, Troy has thrown only one interception in three Super Bowl games.

"I don't have many bad memories from the Super Bowl," says Troy. No kidding!

SCOUTING REPORT

Born: November 21, 1966, in West Covina, California
Career Stats (through 1997): Completed 62 percent of passes for 129 TDs in nine seasons with the Dallas Cowboys. All-time leader for Cowboys in passing attempts, completions, and passing yards. Named to six Pro Bowls.
Super Bowl Stats (through 1998): Completed 56 of 80 passes for 689 yards and five TDs in three games (1993, '94, '96). Was MVP of '93 Super Bowl.

QUICK

Top 10 Troy has thrown for 300 or more yards in a game 10 different times, and four times in the post-season.
Mr. Accuracy Troy holds the Super Bowl career record for highest completion percentage. He has completed 70 percent of his passes.
Long Ball The record for the longest completed pass in the post-season is held by Troy. It was a 94-yarder to Alvin Harper in an NFC divisional playoff game in January 1995.
Mr. Cowboy Troy has started more games at quarterback (142) for the Cowboys than anyone else.

Emmitt Smith

SUPER PLAYERS

Emmitt is often in a rush — to score!

WALTER IOOSS, JR./SPORTS ILLUSTRATED

The Buffalo Bills never knew what hit them. After leading the Dallas Cowboys 13–6 at halftime of Super Bowl XXVIII (1994), the Bills were off to a good start.

Then they ran into a steamroller named Emmitt Smith. During halftime, the Cowboys' star running back told offensive coordinator Norv Turner, "Get me the ball." That's just what the Cowboys did.

After halftime, the Cowboys tied the game on a fumble recovery that was run in for a TD. Then they began giving the ball to Emmitt. And they kept giving it to him. He carried *six straight times* for 46 yards on the team's first offensive drive of the second half. After a one-play break, Emmitt got the call again. He ran for a 15-yard touchdown to give the Cowboys a 20–13 lead.

In the fourth quarter, Emmitt carried the ball six more times in a 10-play drive. He scored a one-yard TD on fourth down to give the Cowboys a 27–13 lead. Emmitt finished the game with 30 carries for 132 yards and two touchdowns. He had clearly been key in the 30–13 Dallas victory.

It was not the first time Emmitt had put on a Super Bowl show. The year before that, also against the Bills, he rushed 22 times for 108 yards and one TD. Dallas won big: 52–17!

The Cowboys didn't make the Super Bowl in 1995, but they were back in 1996. Emmitt had two TDs, as Dallas beat the Pittsburgh Steelers, 27–17. His five rushing touchdowns is a Super Bowl career record. "He has as much pride as any player," said Dallas coach Jimmy Johnson. "That's why he's best at what he does."

KICKS

Mr. Post-Season Emmitt holds the record for most post-season TDs (20), most points (120), and most 100-yard rushing games (7).

Ball Carrier Through the 1997 season, the Cowboys were 75–12 when Emmitt carried the ball 20 or more times in a game.

TD Man I In 1995, Emmitt set the NFL single-season record for TDs (25).

TD Man II Emmitt had 10 TDs in each of his first seven seasons in the NFL. Hall of Famer Jim Brown is the only other NFL player to do that.

SCOUTING REPORT

Born: May 15, 1969, in Pensacola, Florida

Career Stats (through 1997): Rushed for 11,234 yards and 112 TDs on 2,595 carries in eight seasons with the Dallas Cowboys. Has four NFL rushing titles. Named the NFL's 1993 MVP.

Super Bowl Stats (through 1998): Rushed 70 times for 289 yards and a record five touchdowns in three games (1993, '94, '96). Named MVP of 1994 game.

15

Steve Young

It is never easy to follow a legend. But that's what Steve Young did in 1991 when he took over as quarterback of the San Francisco 49ers. Before Steve, Joe Montana *(see page 10)* was the 49ers quarterback. Joe may be the greatest quarterback of all time. He was especially great when it came to playing in the Super Bowl. He led the 49ers to four Super Bowl wins!

So Steve was under a lot of pressure to lead the team to a Super Bowl victory. He had been named the NFL's Most Valuable Player in 1992 but had failed to get the 49ers to the Super Bowl. In 1992 and 1993, the team had lost to the Dallas Cowboys in the NFC Championship game.

"It weighs on me as a part of this team," Steve told the *San Francisco Chronicle*. The San Francisco fans complained that Steve couldn't win important games.

But in January 1995, Steve and the 49ers finally made it. They beat the Cowboys, 38–28, for the NFC title and a trip to the Super Bowl.

The Niners then faced the San Diego Chargers in Super Bowl XXIX, in Miami, Florida. Steve didn't waste any time in Miami. Less than a minute and a half into the game, in just his third play, Steve threw a 44-yard touchdown pass to receiving star Jerry Rice *(see page 11)*. No team had ever scored that quickly in a Super Bowl! Less than four minutes later, Steve threw a 51-yard touchdown pass to running back Ricky Watters. Steve threw two more touchdown passes before halftime. The 49ers led, 28–10.

Steve was just as good in the second half. He threw two more touchdown passes to Jerry. Steve even led the 49ers in rushing, with 49 yards on five attempts. San Francisco won, 49–26. Steve was named MVP.

Steve saluted those who believed he would win the Big One.

SCOUTING REPORT

Born: October 11, 1961, in Salt Lake City, Utah

Career Stats (through 1997): Completed 64.8 percent of his passes for 193 TDs in 13 seasons with the Tampa Bay Buccaneers and San Francisco. Named NFL Player of the Year in 1992 *and* 1994. Selected to six Pro Bowls.

Super Bowl Stats (through 1998): Completed 26 of 39 passes for 345 yards and six touchdowns in two games; MVP of Super Bowl XXIX (1995).

Cool Fact: Steve graduated from Brigham Young University in 1984 and earned his law degree there in 1994. The school is named after his great-great-great-grandfather.

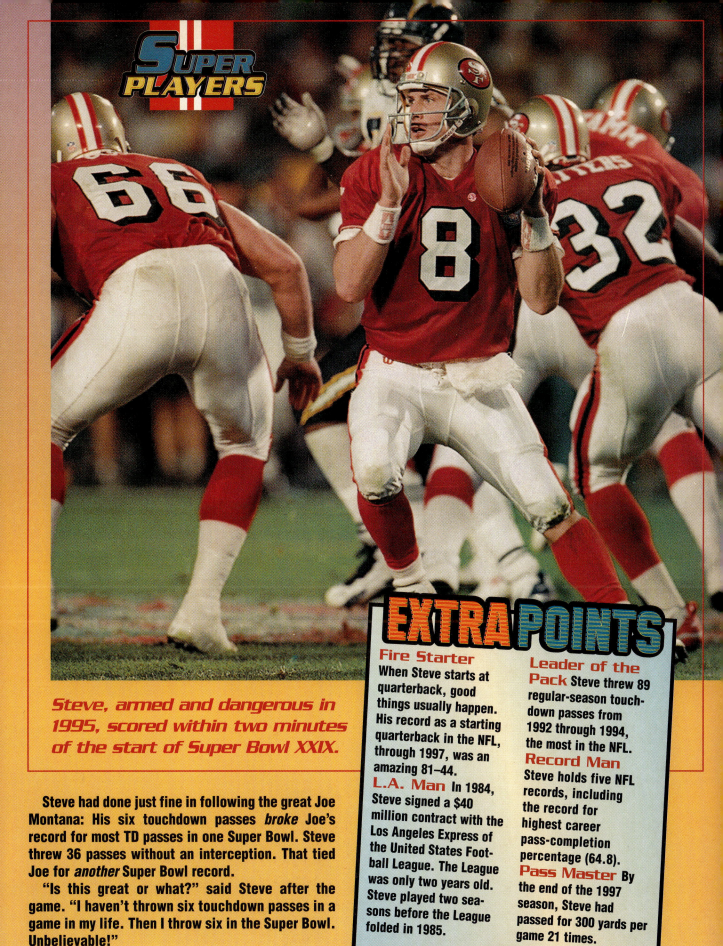

SUPER PLAYERS

Steve, armed and dangerous in 1995, scored within two minutes of the start of Super Bowl XXIX.

Steve had done just fine in following the great Joe Montana: His six touchdown passes *broke* Joe's record for most TD passes in one Super Bowl. Steve threw 36 passes without an interception. That tied Joe for *another* Super Bowl record.

"Is this great or what?" said Steve after the game. "I haven't thrown six touchdown passes in a game in my life. Then I throw six in the Super Bowl. Unbelievable!"

EXTRA POINTS

Fire Starter When Steve starts at quarterback, good things usually happen. His record as a starting quarterback in the NFL, through 1997, was an amazing 81–44.

L.A. Man In 1984, Steve signed a $40 million contract with the Los Angeles Express of the United States Football League. The League was only two years old. Steve played two seasons before the League folded in 1985.

Leader of the Pack Steve threw 89 regular-season touchdown passes from 1992 through 1994, the most in the NFL.

Record Man Steve holds five NFL records, including the record for highest career pass-completion percentage (64.8).

Pass Master By the end of the 1997 season, Steve had passed for 300 yards per game 21 times.

BRETT FAVRE

The Green Bay Packer quarterback felt right at home for

Super Bowl XXXI. After all, Brett Favre's hometown of Kiln, Mississippi, is only about one hour's drive away from the Louisiana Superdome, in New Orleans, where the Packers were to play the January 1997 game against the New England Patriots. Brett had played games in the Superdome on seven different occasions before that Super Bowl. He had never lost there.

So Brett felt at home. But he didn't feel *well* in the days leading up to the Big Game. He could hardly get out of bed

EXTRA POINTS

Leader of Pack
In just six seasons, through 1997, Brett had thrown more TD passes (182) than anyone else in team history.

A Cool Guy Brett warms up when it gets cold. Through the 1997-98 season, he had a perfect 22–0 record (including the post-season) when the game-time temperature was below 35 degrees.

Touchdown Man
Brett is the only NFL quarterback ever to throw at least 30 TD passes in each of four straight seasons. He did it in 1994-97.

Speed Racer
Brett became the second-fastest NFL quarterback to throw for 20,000 career yards. He did it in 86 games. Miami Dolphin QB Dan Marino did it in 74 games.

TOM DIPACE

because of a terrible bout with the flu. "I was worried," says Brett. "I waited my whole life to play in [the Super Bowl], and now I wasn't going to be healthy." But when he woke up on Super Bowl Sunday, Brett was ready to go.

Brett wasted little time putting points on the scoreboard. On the Packers' second play, he fired a 54-yard touchdown pass to wide receiver Andre Rison. Then, with the Patriots leading 14–10 at the beginning of the second quarter, Brett made a great call. He threw a perfect pass to wideout Antonio Freeman. Antonio ran past the Patriot defenders for an 81-yard touchdown. It was the longest passing play in Super Bowl history.

But Brett was not done. With 1:11 left in the second quarter, he scored from the two-yard line to give the Packers a 27–14 lead. The Packers went on to win the game, 35–21.

"It would be great to win anywhere," said Brett after the game. "But being so close to home . . . I don't believe this could be better."

SCOUTING REPORT

Born: October 10, 1969, in Gulfport, Mississippi

Career Stats (through 1997): Completed 61.5 percent of his passes for 182 TDs over seven seasons with the Falcons and Packers. First player to win MVP award three times in a row.

Super Bowl Stats (through 1998): Completed 39 of 69 passes for 502 yards, five TDs (plus 1 rushing) in two games.

Brett had reason to celebrate after the Super Bowl in 1997. The Packers won, 35–21, and he threw the longest pass in Super Bowl history.

PETER READ MILLER/SPORTS ILLUSTRATED

TERRELL DAVIS

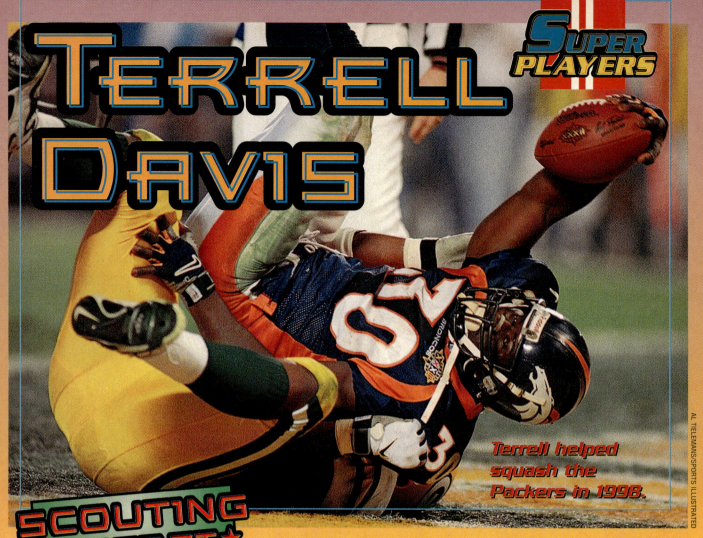

Terrell helped squash the Packers in 1998.

SCOUTING REPORT

Born: October 28, 1972, in San Diego, California

Career Stats (through 1997): Rushed for 4,405 yards overall and scored 38 touchdowns in three seasons with Denver. Rushed for 2,331 yards during the 1997 regular and post-season — more than any running back in NFL history. Named to two Pro Bowls.

Super Bowl Stats (through 1998): Was named Super Bowl MVP after rushing for 157 yards and scoring three touchdowns in Super Bowl XXXII, in 1998.

Cool Fact: Terrell was a hometown hero when we won the MVP award at Super Bowl XXXII, in San Diego, California.

Running back Terrell Davis of the Denver Broncos is great

at carrying the ball. He did it a lot in the 1997-98 season. He did it in the regular season, he did it in the post-season, and he did it in the Super Bowl. Nothing can stop Terrell from carrying the ball — not even a terrible headache that is so bad he can't see straight.

In Super Bowl XXXII, against the Green Bay Packers, Terrell took a blow to the head late in the first quarter. After the collision, Terrell began to feel woozy. He even blacked out for a few seconds. When he came to, his vision was blurry. Then Terrell began to get a really bad headache called a *migraine*. A migraine is a pounding headache that strikes suddenly. Terrell has been getting migraines since he was 7 years old.

WALTER IOOSS, JR./SPORTS ILLUSTRATED

Terrell was in a rush to score three TDs in Super Bowl XXXII.

"I couldn't see," says Terrell. "I thought, 'Man! Not at the Super Bowl.'"

Teammate Shannon Sharpe noticed something was wrong. He told Terrell to go to the sideline. Terrell spent most of the first half receiving oxygen and taking medication for his pain. "It took awhile," Terrell says. "But when I came back from halftime, my vision was back and I knew I was going to be okay."

Terrell returned to the game for the start of the third quarter. He fumbled the ball on his first carry. But for the rest of the game, the only pain being felt was by the Packer defense! In the second half, Terrell ran for 93 yards and two touchdowns. The Broncos won, 31–24, and Terrell finished with 157 yards and three touchdowns, even though he missed most of the second quarter. He was named the Super Bowl MVP!

"I think the Packers have migraines now," Terrell said afterward.

No doubt, they think he's a pain!

EXTRA POINTS

What a Steal
The Broncos selected Terrell in the sixth round of the 1995 NFL draft. He was the 196th overall player selected that year. There were *20* running backs selected ahead of Terrell.

Freshman Sensation Terrell rushed for 1,117 yards in his rookie season. He is the lowest drafted rookie in NFL history to rush for 1,000 yards.

Everywhere Man Terrell played six different positions on his high school football team, including nose guard.

Workhorse
In 1997, Terrell rushed for more yards (2,331, including the post-season) and carried the ball more times (481 times, including the post-season) in one season than any other running back in NFL history.

Quick Study
After only three seasons with the Broncos, Terrell already held 47 Bronco records, including 19 post-season records.

King of the AFC
Terrell led the AFC in rushing in the 1996 and 1997 seasons. In 1996, he rushed for 1,538 yards and 13 touchdowns on 345 carries. In 1997, he finished with 1,750 yards and scored 15 TDs on 369 carries.

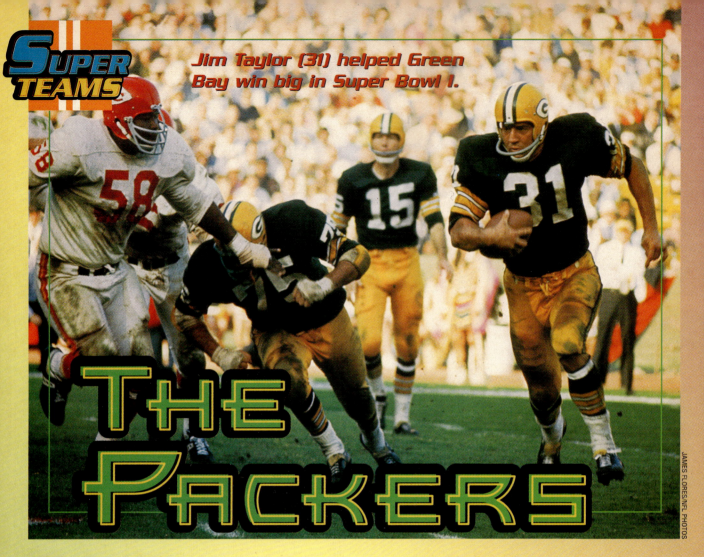

Jim Taylor (31) helped Green Bay win big in Super Bowl I.

The Packers

What players come to mind when you think

of the Green Bay Packers? Probably quarterback Brett Favre and monster defensive end Reggie White, right? Brett and Reggie led the Packers to two straight Super Bowl appearances, in 1997 and 1998. In the 1997 game, the Packers beat the New England Patriots, 35–21, in Super Bowl XXXI. From 1995 through 1997, Green Bay won 37 games and lost only 11. Not bad.

But as good as the Packers are these days, the Packers of the 1960's were even better. They were led by a tough-as-nails coach named Vince Lombardi, a pinpoint passer named Bart Starr *(see page 4),* and great stars like running back Jim Taylor and linebacker Ray Nitschke. Beginning in 1961, they won five NFL titles in seven years!

The Packers also won the first two Super Bowl games. They trounced the Kansas City Chiefs, 35–10, in Super Bowl I, and whipped the Oakland Raiders, 33–14, in Super Bowl II. "You will make mistakes," Coach Lombardi once said, "but not many if you want to play for the Green Bay Packers."

And that's why Green Bay is called Titletown U.S.A.

Late in the third quarter of Super Bowl XXXI, in 1997, the New England Patriots had cut the Packers' lead to 27–21. Desmond Howard, the Green Bay Packer speedy kick returner, fielded the Patriots kickoff at his own 1-yard line. He burst up the middle and kept going all the way to the end zone. His 99-yard kickoff return was the longest in Super Bowl history!

The Packers won, 35–21. Desmond returned a Super Bowl record of 244 yards and became the first special-teams player to be voted the Super Bowl MVP.

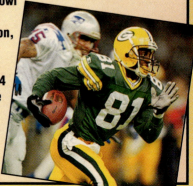

SUPER TEAMS

THE DOLPHINS

One word best describes the 1972 Dolphins: Perfect!

Have you ever heard

the expression nobody's perfect? Well, in 1972, the Miami Dolphins *were* perfect. They played 14 games in the regular season and three in the post-season — and won every game! The Dolphins' 17–0 season was the first perfect season in NFL history.

In 1974, the Dolphins became the first team to play in three Super Bowls in a row. They lost to the Dallas Cowboys, 24–3, in 1972. But they won the next two Super Bowls, beating the Washington Redskins, 14–7, and the Minnesota Vikings, 24–7.

Quarterback Bob Griese *(right)* and wide receiver Paul Warfield took care of the passing game. Running backs Larry Csonka, Mercury Morris, and Jim Kiick trampled opponents. The defense was nicknamed the No Name Defense because there were no superstars on the squad. But they did the job!

HERO

Miami Dolphins starting quarterback **Bob Griese** had a tough year in 1972. He fractured his ankle in the fifth game of the season and missed the rest of the regular season. But the Dolphins hadn't suffered as much as Bob had. Earl Morrall replaced Bob and led Miami to nine wins in a row!

When the Dolphins made it to the Super Bowl, coach Don Shula had to make a difficult decision. Which quarterback should he start: Earl or Bob?

Coach Shula decided to go with Bob. It turned out to be a great choice. Bob completed 8 of 11 passes for 88 yards and threw a touchdown pass in the 14–7 win. It was the perfect end to a perfect season. The Dolphins finished with a record of 17 wins and no losses — thanks to *both* quarterbacks!

SUPER TEAMS

The Steelers ruled the NFL in the 1970's.

THE STEELERS

RICHARD PILLING/NFL PHOTOS

During the 1970's, the Pittsburgh Steelers seemed to have more stars than the solar system. They were led on offense by future Hall of Fame quarterback Terry Bradshaw *(see page 8)*, running backs Franco Harris *(page 9)* and Rocky Bleier, and wide receivers Lynn Swann *(page 29)* and John Stallworth. They also had an awesome defense *(see box, right)*.

These stars helped the Steelers become the first NFL team to win the Super Bowl four times. They won those games in a six-year span, winning back-to-back titles in 1975 and 1976, and again in 1979 and 1980.

"All the Steelers, we loved to win," said Terry. You can't argue with Terry!

HEROES

In the 1970's, the Pittsburgh Steeler defense was called **The Steel Curtain**. Like the Iron Curtain that once separated communist Europe from the rest of the world, this curtain kept everything out!

In Super Bowl IX (1975), L.C. Greenwood, "Mean" Joe Greene, Jack Lambert, Mel Blount, Donnie Shell, and their defensive teammates held the Minnesota Vikings to just 17 yards rushing for the game. Pittsburgh won, 16–6.

In Super Bowl XIV (1980), the Los Angeles Rams trailed by only five points when linebacker Jack Lambert intercepted a pass in the fourth quarter. The play saved the day for the Steelers. They won the game, 31–19.

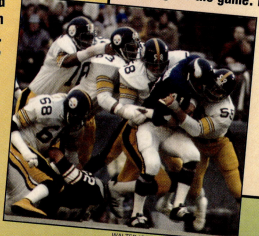

WALTER IOOSS, JR/SPORTS ILLUSTRATED

THE REDSKINS

SuperTEAMS

PAUL JASIENSKI

Mark Rypien (top, right) led the Skins in Super Bowl XXVI.

HERO

The Washington Redskins were expected to have trouble scoring against the Miami Dolphins in Super Bowl XVII (1983). The Dolphins had the best defense in the NFL. But the Redskins had a secret weapon: 230-pound running back **John Riggins!**

Against the Dolphins, John rushed for 166 yards on 38 carries. That set two Super Bowl records and earned him the MVP.

One of John's carries turned the game around. The Redskins were losing, 17–13, in the fourth quarter. It was fourth down, with one yard to go. The Redskins were on the Dolphin 43-yard line. They gave the ball to John, and he ran the ball into the end zone!

The touchdown gave the Redskins their first lead of the game. They went on to win, 27–17. It was the team's first Super Bowl win. And it was a big one!

WALTER IOOSS, JR./SPORTS ILLUSTRATED

All that work and no

payoff! The Washington Redskins made the NFL playoffs in five of six seasons in the 1970's. But they played in only one Super Bowl and lost. In 1973, the Skins lost Super Bowl VII to the Miami Dolphins, 14–7.

Ten years later, led by John Riggins *(see "Hero," left)*, they beat the Dolphins, 27–17. It was the first of three Super Bowl titles for Washington.

In Super Bowl XXII (1988), quarterback Doug Williams threw four touchdown passes in the second quarter. Running back Timmy Smith set a rushing record of 204 yards. The Skins beat the Denver Broncos, 42–10.

Four years later, quarterback Mark Rypien led Washington to victory in Super Bowl XXVI. Mark threw for 292 yards and two touchdowns to defeat the Buffalo Bills, 37–24.

SUPER TEAMS

The 49ers have celebrated many Super Bowl victories.

THE 49ers

HERO

John Taylor, a wide receiver for the San Francisco 49ers, had only one catch in Super Bowl XXIII (1989). But what a catch! It turned around the game in its final minute.

The 49ers were trailing the Cincinnati Bengals, 16–13, with less than a minute to play. On a second down from the Bengal 10-yard line, 49er quarterback Joe Montana dropped back to pass. The pass was supposed to go to running back Roger Craig, but Roger had two guys covering him!

John had escaped his coverage and was open in the end zone. He faked to the outside, then darted to the middle. "All I could think was 'Catch the ball,'" he said.

That's just what John did *(right)*. The TD catch with 34 seconds left in the game helped the 49ers to a 20–16 win, and their third title. It was the first time that a Super Bowl had been decided on a touchdown in the final minute of play.

Talk about a super team!

Through 1998, the San Francisco 49ers had a perfect Super Bowl record: 5–0. Only three other teams have never lost the NFL's biggest game. And none of those have won five!

Led by Joe Montana *(see page 10)*, one of the greatest quarterbacks ever, the 49ers won the Super Bowl four times between 1982 and 1990. In 1991, Steve Young *(page 16)* replaced Joe. In 1995, he led the team to another *super* win!

Other great 49er players include wide receivers Dwight Clark and Jerry Rice *(page 11)*, running backs Ricky Watters and Roger Craig, and kicker Ray Wersching.

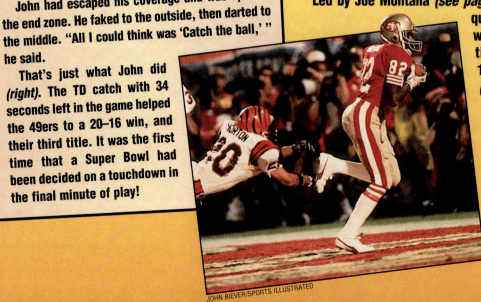

THE COWBOYS

SUPER TEAMS

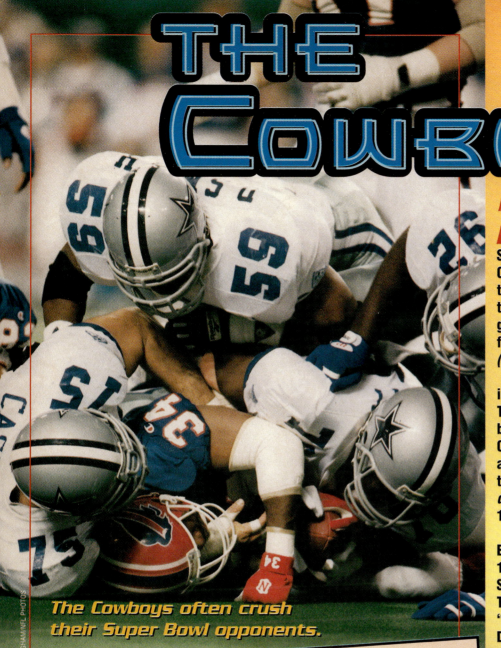

The Cowboys often crush their Super Bowl opponents.

No team has played in more

Super Bowl games than the Dallas Cowboys. Between 1971 and 1996, they played in the Big Game eight times! They won five of those games. The only other team to win five is the San Francisco 49ers *(see opposite page).*

Three of the Cowboys' wins came in the 1990's. Led by quarterback Troy Aikman *(page 14)* and running back Emmitt Smith *(page 15)*, the Cowboys won two straight in 1993 and 1994, and a third in 1996. And they didn't just win — Dallas *dominated*, outscoring opponents 109–47 in the three games!

The Cowboys' other five Super Bowl appearances were in the 1970's. Quarterback Roger Staubach *(page 6)*, running back Tony Dorsett, and defensive end Ed "Too Tall" Jones were among the Dallas stars then. (Ed got his nickname because he was 6' 9" tall!)

The Dallas Cowboys had plenty of star players: Troy Aikman, Emmitt Smith, Deion Sanders, Larry Brown . . . Larry who?

That's right. The speedy cornerback *(right)* upstaged his more famous teammates at Super Bowl XXX (1996). Larry intercepted two passes in the second half to stop the Pittsburgh Steelers. He became only the sixth defensive player named Super Bowl MVP.

Dallas was leading, 13–7, in the third quarter. Larry intercepted a pass at the Dallas 38-yard line. He ran it 20 yards. Two plays later, the Cowboys scored for a 20–7 lead.

Larry's second interception came with just over four minutes left. The Cowboys' lead was down to three points, and Pittsburgh had the ball. But Larry intercepted a pass at the Steeler 39 and returned it to the 6. Emmitt Smith scored two plays later to seal the 27–17 victory for the Cowboys.

SUPER MOMENTS 1971

The Colts waited and then Jim (below) celebrated his winning kick.

WALTER IOOSS, JR./SPORTS ILLUSTRATED

Up and Over!

Before Super Bowl V, rookie kicker Jim O'Brien had a dream. He dreamed that someone kicked a game-winning field goal but he couldn't tell if *he* did it or it was Dallas Cowboy kicker Mike Clark!

When the real game was played, Jim had the chance the find out whose kick would win the game. Late in the fourth quarter, the score was tied at 13. With 1:09 left in the game, Baltimore linebacker Mike Curtis intercepted a pass at the Dallas 41-yard line and ran the ball back to the Dallas 28.

There were just five seconds left on the clock when Jim ran onto the field to try to kick a 32-yard field goal. If he made it, the Colts would win the Super Bowl!

"When we lined up for the winning field goal, the Dallas linemen were yelling at me, trying to distract me," says Jim.

Then Jim recalled that one of his teammates, Billy Ray Smith, would yell at him in practice to prepare him for distractions. So Jim pretended that it was Billy Ray yelling instead of the Cowboy defenders.

Jim's little trick worked. The kick sailed straight through the uprights. Jim jumped up in the air. "It was probably the best kick I ever kicked in my life," says Jim.

DICK RAPHAEL/NFL PHOTOS

SCOUTING REPORT

Name: Jim O'Brien
Born: February 2, 1947, in El Paso, Texas
Career Stats: Made 60 of 108 field goals in four seasons (1970-73) with the Baltimore Colts and Detroit Lions.
Super Bowl Stats: Made one of two field goals and one of two extra points in Super Bowl V.
Cool Fact: Jim also played receiver during his career. He averaged 21.8 yards per catch (14 receptions for 305 yards) and scored two touchdowns.

SWANN DIVE

SUPER MOMENTS 1976

In the days leading up to Super Bowl X, Pittsburgh Steeler wide receiver Lynn Swann was dropping passes in practice. Two weeks earlier, he had suffered a concussion from a hard hit to the head in the AFC Championship game. Lynn was having trouble concentrating. Would he even be able to play in the Super Bowl?

Lynn's answer to that question was loud and clear: *Yes!* In the first quarter, Lynn and Dallas Cowboy cornerback Mark Washington ran down the sideline, fighting for the ball. Lynn nabbed it for a 32-yard gain.

Lynn's most spectacular catch of the game came near the end of the second quarter. Lynn had to leap into the air and, once again, tip the ball away from Mark Washington. As both players fell to the ground *(right)*, Lynn was able to hold on to the ball for a 53-yard gain.

Lynn wasn't done. With 3:02 left in the game, Lynn caught a long pass at the Dallas five-yard line. He stumbled into the end zone for the touchdown. The 63-yard play sealed the Steelers' 21–17 win. Lynn caught four passes for 161 yards and was voted the game's MVP.

Lynn said afterward the passing game was really clicking. How about the *catching* game?

SCOUTING REPORT

Name: Lynn Swann
Born: March 7, 1952, in Alcoa, Tennessee
Career Stats: Caught 336 passes for 5,462 yards and 51 TDs in nine seasons (1974-82) with the Pittsburgh Steelers.
Super Bowl Stats: Caught 16 passes for 364 yards and three touchdowns in four Super Bowls (1975, '76, '79, '80).
Cool Fact: Lynn Swann held the record for most career Super Bowl receiving yards until Jerry Rice broke that record in 1995.

Lynn's sore head didn't keep his hands from hauling in the ball in Super Bowl X.

HEINZ KLUETMEIER/SPORTS ILLUSTRATED

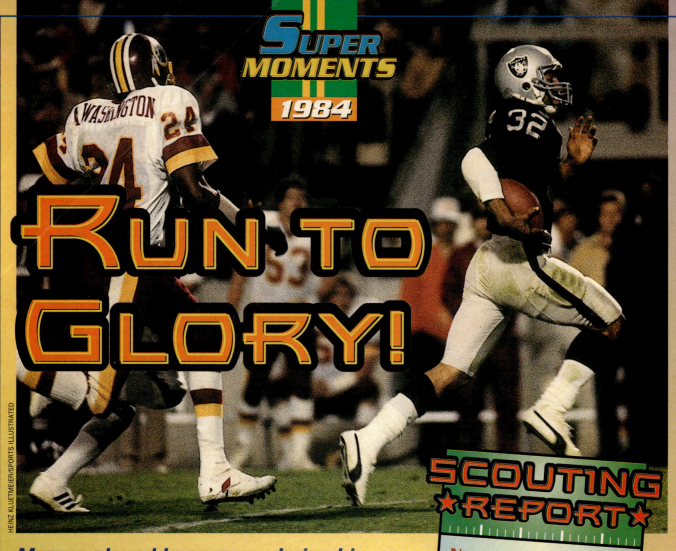

Super Moments 1984

Run to Glory!

Marcus played keep-away during his amazing 74-yard touchdown run.

Marcus Allen really didn't have to do it. His team, the

Los Angeles Raiders, was already beating the Washington Redskins in Super Bowl XVIII (1984), 28–9. Still, with 12 seconds left in the third quarter, the nimble running back pulled off one of the most amazing plays in the history of the Super Bowl.

It started when Marcus took a handoff from Raider quarterback Jim Plunkett at L.A.'s 26-yard line. Marcus darted to his left. But a gang of Redskin defenders loomed in front of him. So Marcus hit the brakes and headed in the opposite direction. He spotted an opening in the middle of the field and dashed through it!

Once Marcus was in the clear, the Redskin defenders were no match for him. He ended up with a 74-yard touchdown run — the longest run from scrimmage in Super Bowl history!

That was Marcus's second touchdown of the game. He finished with a total of 191 yards rushing and was the game's MVP.

"It was the best run I've had in the NFL," said Marcus. "I didn't think of what to do on the run. I just let my instincts take over."

Scouting Report

Name: Marcus Allen
Born: March 26, 1960, in San Diego, California
Career Stats: Rushed for 12,243 yards, caught 587 passes for 5,411 yards, and scored 145 touchdowns in 16 seasons (1982-97) with the L.A. Raiders and Kansas City Chiefs. Named NFL Rookie of the Year in 1982 and NFL Player of the Year in '85.
Super Bowl Stats: Rushed for 191 yards and two touchdowns on 20 carries in one game (Super Bowl XVIII). Holds record for longest touchdown run (74 yards). Named Super Bowl MVP.
Fast Fact: Marcus is the first running back in NFL history to run for more than 10,000 yards and catch passes for more than 5,000 yards.

HEINZ KLUETMEIER/SPORTS ILLUSTRATED

SCOUTING ★ REPORT ★

Name: William Perry
Born: December 16, 1962, in Aiken, South Carolina
Career Stats: Had 29.5 sacks and scored three TDs in 10 seasons (1985-94) with the Chicago Bears and Philadelphia Eagles.
Super Bowl Stats: Scored a touchdown in Super Bowl XX (1986) on a one-yard run.
Cool Fact: William was nicknamed the "Refrigerator" after a teammate at Clemson University had to squeeze past him to get onto an elevator.

SUPER MOMENTS 1986

The "Refrigerator"— all 300+ pounds of him — scored on this run.

RICHARD PILLING/NFL PHOTOS

PERRY'S PLUNGE

Imagine trying to tackle a 335-pound running back. Most running backs weigh about 200 pounds. In Super Bowl XX (1986), the Chicago Bears used one who weighed 135 pounds more than that! The New England Patriots didn't have a chance.

The Bears had a first down on the one-yard line late in the third quarter. They were leading 37-3. The Bears sent out rookie defensive tackle William "Refrigerator" Perry to carry the ball.

Tackles are huge and almost never replace speedy running backs. But during a game earlier in the season, Chicago coach Mike Ditka asked William to line up at running back. William scored a touchdown!

Still, this was the Super Bowl.

The Fridge took the handoff and plowed through Patriot linebacker Larry McGrew. Touchdown! The Bears went on to win the game, 46–10. After that, William ran the ball just three more times in his career, for a loss of two yards.

"What I dreamed of as a boy was to play in the Super Bowl," William said after the game. "To score a touchdown in the Super Bowl — I'm overwhelmed by it."

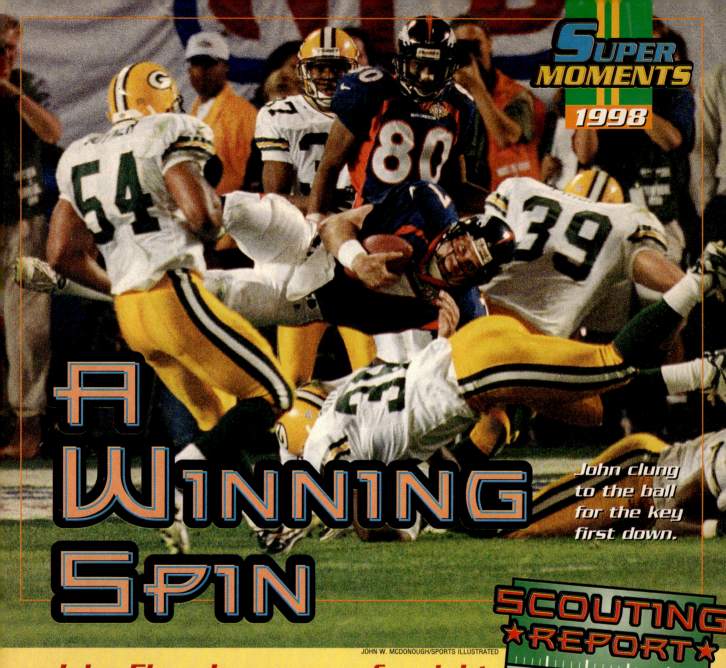

SUPER MOMENTS 1998

A Winning Spin

John clung to the ball for the key first down.

JOHN W. MCDONOUGH/SPORTS ILLUSTRATED

John Elway's cannon of a right arm has helped the quarterback win plenty of games for the Denver Broncos. But against the Green Bay Packers in Super Bowl XXXII, it was John's *legs* that helped the Broncos become Super Bowl champions.

The teams were tied at 17–17 in the third quarter when John's big moment came. With his team facing a third down and six yards to go from the Green Bay 12-yard line, John knew he *had* to find a way to get a first down. But when he dropped back to pass on the play, he could not find any open receivers to throw to. He decided to make a run for it.

John sprinted into the open field, where he was met by Packer safety LeRoy Butler. The two players collided and John spun into the air like a helicopter. When John finally landed, the Broncos had a first down at the Green Bay four-yard line. Two plays later, Terrell Davis scored to put the Broncos ahead. They would go on to win the game by a score of 31–24. The win was sweeter than usual. It was the first time in four tries that John had won the Super Bowl!

SCOUTING REPORT

Name: John Elway
Born: June 28, 1960, in Port Angeles, Washington
Career Stats (through 1997): Completed 56.8 percent of his passes for 278 touchdowns from 1983 through 1997. Named to six Pro Bowls.
Super Bowl Stats (through 1998): Completed 58 of 123 passes for 792 yards and two touchdowns in four Super Bowls (1982, '88, '90, '98).
Cool Fact: John ranks second on the NFL's all-time list for career passing yards.